OUT OF THE RAIN

Glyn Maxwell was born in 1962 in Welwyn Garden City, the second son of a scientist and an actress. After reading English at Oxford, he worked in Geneva. In 1987 he won a major scholarship in poetry and playwriting at Boston University, and has since worked as a freelance writer and publisher's editor. His first collection *Tale of the Mayor's Son* (Bloodaxe Books, 1990), was a Poetry Book Society Choice, and was shortlisted for the *Mail on Sunday* / John Llewellyn Rhys Prize and the *Sunday Times* Young Writer's Award. He won an Eric Gregory Award for his poetry in 1991.

His second collection, *Out of the Rain* (Bloodaxe Books, 1992), is a Poetry Book Society Recommendation. As well as being a prolific poet, he writes and acts in plays, and stages productions of his verse-plays in his own back garden in Welwyn Garden City.

OUT OF THE RAIN

Glyn Maxwell

for Martin with best wishes in hope it a rhyme for Blaenau ffestiniog ...

BLOODAXE BOOKS

ISBN: 1 85224 193 4

First published 1992 by
Bloodaxe Books Ltd,
P.O. Box 1SN,
Newcastle upon Tyne NE99 1SN.

Bloodaxe Books Ltd acknowledges
the financial assistance of Northern Arts.

Cover reproduction by V & H Reprographics, Newcastle upon Tyne.

Cover printing by J. Thomson Colour Printers Ltd, Glasgow.

Printed in Great Britain by
Bell & Bain Limited, Glasgow, Scotland.

I wish, I wish, I wish in vain
That we could sit simply in that room again,
Ten thousand dollars at the drop of a hat,
I'd give it all gladly if our lives could be like that.

FROM 'Bob Dylan's Dream'

Acknowledgements

Acknowledgements are due to the editors of the following publications in which some of these poems first appeared: *Atlantic Monthly* (USA), *Border Country* (Woodwind/West Midlands Arts, 1991), *Illuminations, London Review of Books, Manhattan Review* (USA), New Writing, vol. 1 (Minerva/British Council, 1992), *Oxford Poetry, People to People, Poetry Review, The Rialto, Soho Square IV* (Bloomsbury, 1991), *The Spectator, Stand, Times Literary Supplement*, and *Verse*.

'Sport Story of a Winner' was read on *Wordworks* (Tyne Tees Television) and published in the *Wordworks* anthology (Bloodaxe Books/Tyne Tees Television, 1992).

Contents

I. OUT OF THE RAIN

Errand Boy

To amble on on the brightening, clouding
pavement to happen to pass whom he wants,
        innocently, to pass involves
passing his home with feigned indifference
and moving on, nowhere left to be heading.

She is the brown bare-armed au pair,
her charges holding her hands. Though he really
        means his major smile at them,
it is all in his own and other way fairly
for her, and their voices are English and clear

as they fade, hers neither as it also fades.
And now he's stuck on an imaginary errand, which
        seems to be suddenly unimportant
from the way he slows down and checks his watch
then monitors interesting forming clouds.

War Hero

Where recollections end,
    step finally from the land
and into the white before like the masked birdman,
a boy is bound to appear:
    growing, hurrying here
over the hot dry grass towards his grandad.

He, who fought on the Somme,
    wanted to see the same
storm damage, down the road on a meadow,
as did this boy of five.
    The sky all blue above.
Was there a storm? morning enquiring. Never.

I caught him up on the road.
    'Look at the oak,' he said,
and sure enough it was peeled to the root by lightning
we'd both seen. Its scar
    was fierce white. Nowhere
could we see the bark tracked clean off with a fork.

He wouldn't touch the sore.
    'Reckon it's hot there.'
Anything else he reckoned or said about it
he carried onto his flight,
    climbing, level in sunlight,
to Lancashire summers beyond the hideous river.

We Are Off to See the Wizard

A young man, I am on a train in Montana,
    The dark late, the view
Without home or horizon, the air some orange.
I am talking to nobody, looking at nothing.
    I have never met you.

The clouds part in a west before all darkness:
    A yellow hole of sundown,
And through the light-parade at the cocktail hour
They have on this tall train I hear coming
    The name of the next town,

Havre, and the immediate announcement
    Of somewhere up ahead
A true tornado, either to east or west:
Then a little girl crying out 'Oz!' and 'I think I
    Saw it!' a boy just said.

I talk to nobody, look at nothing, I drink
    Only, and I wonder:
Whose horizon and is it ours it is riding
Along, the lassooing Quick-As-Wind, the Witch,
    The Worse-Than-Thunder?

This cliffhanger turns to the cartoon cliffhanger:
    The galloping in thin air,
The ground gone, the drop forever, the toms
Rolling until I realise and gulp,
    Have to, get there.

La Brea

Los Angeles. So just
guess what I saw: not the dust
or the wide jammed road, not that. And not
the park where enormous playthings eat

the shouting children. No, and the glass white
televised cathedral? – that
was a sight seen for the sin-
gle flashed moment, and gone.

I saw the tar-pits at La Brea,
where a dark endowed museum squats, and where
the thick blots of lake are watched,
and the haired replicas stroked and touched

by kiddies. There's a tour:
the intelligible stone, the Short-Faced Bear,
the Dire Wolf, American Lion and Mastodon,
and Man with not much brain.

Well they did all make a dumb
choice that day! But my day was warm
and fascinating. Try to see these
tar-pits, in La Brea, in Los Angeles.

The Day After Christmas

The day after Christmas he awoke,
Where a shuddering soaking weather
Ran its worst outside and his blood was thinned
And watery with the waking hours past.

Friends had gone from the world
For just a day, and now, he supposed, were back
But how it howled between his room and them,
And how could he begin not to see

The year was in its crisis and would die
In days? He could be its doctor and say '5'.
Or be its priest and stand there with a book.
Or be the one who in this curtained room

Hears the lonely giant who has walked from London
With news of wrongs and violence,
And rattles this upstairs window sobbing
'Right them, sir' over the rain and the silence.

The Fires by the River

Just say you went beside the fires by the river,
in neither night nor day, insofar as
violet and lime were the shades of the air that
        steamed or anchored over
the slurping water, and this was the River Thames
        you somehow knew it.

And people had turned to people of those days,
though moreso, now you walked and heard
the actual cursing, the splattered effluents,
        not far from you in the rose-
grey coloured mud that sloped to the pale Thames
        to be its banks.

Just say the place was a mezzanine or less
up from hell, and who wasn't a thug was a child.
And there was a drug called drug, and a drug that went
        by day in a blue guise;
and there was a boat of cocktailers on the Thames
        staring at this point –

at lolling homes, and clapboard warehouses
shot with mice or riddled with the likes
of Monks and Sikes, who mutter by the wharf –
        skin-crawling passages –
all, just say so, that was real as the Thames
        is, by any life:

what would you do with your clean hands and drowned
feet in the place? Remove them to a room?
Remove them to a room. And sit, forget
        the city-licking sound
of water moving slowly through the Thames
        like years in thought.

EC3

Her heart alert and in on things she walks
quickeningly by my side. Her looks
are mirrored dustily on glass that mirrors
crane and ruin high over her. She *is*
    the Eyecatcher. This *is*
    the real City. Some terrors

for me are terrors for her but look how the dust
of drilled churches skips her with a gust
that blinds old me. I blink into all men
dressed as what they are and were all day
    and were all yesterday
    passing neglecting on, un-

der irredeemable heights of rocking steel.
I'd scurry from so high, or seem to kneel
from gap to remaining gap towards remains.
She guides by this, blonde of a village past,
    glancing noticed past.
    My interested remains

hurry on beside what eyes still go
up, down, up, down hopefully and no,
through one bulb-lit and tiny violet cave,
then out between the vital youngster drunk
    and useless ruin drunk,
    where leaden, beaten love

does with what it has. This *is* the mile
ahead. Abandon stabs at it. These pale
scuttling creatures under the high nod
of the pudgy near-to-dead are in it now.
    We thread on by it now,
    exchange the affecting nod

and pass below, away to our ticking homes.
No nothing in the tallest of my dreams
'll grow as tall as, falling up and down
as that, or hook these red uncrediting eyes
    like the Eyecatcher's eyes
    in the dead east of town.

The Eater

Top of the morning, Dogfood Family!
How's the chicken? How's the chicken?
Haven't you grown? Or have you grown,
here in the average kitchen at noontime
    down in the home, at all?

Bang outside, the bank officials
are conga-dancing and in their pinstripe
this is the life! But it isn't your life
out in the swarming city at crushhour
    dodging humans, is it?

Vacant city – where did they find it?
Blossom of litter as the only car
for a man goes by. When the man goes by
his girl will sulkily catch your eye:
    will you catch hers?

Snow-white shop – how do they do that?
Lamb-white medical knowing and gentle
man, advise her, assure and ask her:
do you desire the best for your children
    and theirs? Well do you?

Take that journey, delight in chocolate,
you won't find anyone else in the world,
lady, only the man, the sweet man
opening doors and suggesting later
    something – what thing?

Short time no see, Dogfood Family!
How's the chicken? How's the chicken?
How have you done it? Have you done it
with love, regardless of time and income
    and me? Who am I?

I am the eater and I am the eater.
These are my seconds and these are my seconds.
Do you understand that? Do you get that,
you out there where the good things grow
    and rot? Or not?

The Uninvited

We did not care muchly who, in the murder,
we turned out to be, providing whoever
used to inhabit the white chalk figure
frozenly pawing the blood-stained sofa
was not one of us but a different dier.

Dazzled colonel, distracted lover,
meddling couple of the library whisper,
cook unpoisoned or ponderous super,
sleuth, inheritor, innocent, actual
killer detected or undetected – it

didn't matter, but not that ended
individual manning the hour
he died in, as we would all one *dies*
man one hour, one mo, one jiffy.
Let us be Anybody other than Body!

But then we'd go on with the game all summer:
the three allowed queries on the hot verandah,
the fib in the gazebo, the starlit rumour,
the twitching curtain and the dim unhelpful
gardener's boy: it would all be explicable

soon in the lounge, and we didn't mind waiting.
No, what we minded was the hairless stranger
who wasn't invited and wouldn't answer
and had no secrets or skeletons either,
and got up later than us, then later

than even the bodies, and never turned in,
or blamed or suspected or guessed the outcome
but always was exiting, vanishing, going,
seen on the lawn – then there were more of them
massing, unarmed, parting when followed,

combing the country but not for a weapon
or corpse or clue, then halting and singing
unknown thunderous hymns to a leader
new on us all at our country party he'd
caught in the act of an act of murder.

Thunder to Thunder

As coffee in the air stains the shredding machine
    and the folded exec is erasing the little tape
as we speak –
    amigo, there'll be no trial, no magazine
    feature, no scam and no scoop next week.

Deliberate big men man the one outgate,
    stabbing at the life of the salaried doll
as she drives by –
    what's in her compact and who's at her tailgate,
    who buys it, to whom does she sob her 'hi'?

Amigo, the traffic locks, thunder to thunder.
    Your friends who'll be shot will be running and shot
but not for lies
    and not in this quarter. The freeway heads under
    a frozen freeway that does likewise.

Four are becoming The Four and hold sway
    steadily upon a desert millions till.
One isn't of straw,
    one doesn't lack a heart, one won't run away,
    one isn't saying 'Skies are blue.' The rest are.

Amigo, you anticipate just conclusions?
    Then steer what craft you can find at a sun
that looks as if it
    hangs in its space unsmeared by pollutions,
    looks like it rises and shines – have it –

for the weak man's standing by the gate in the morning,
    and wire is everywhere. Envisage the wire
away where it leads
    past the penultimate and ultimate warning,
    around a populace it bleeds and bleeds

till the shades electing themselves in the mist
    of morning are guiltless and rosy. Drive up
and let them tell you,
    amigo, they bear both arms and a great past
    here, and it means if they want they kill you.

The Hang of It

Hugh it was who told me, didn't tell me,
Showed me, wouldn't let my hands on his

Cowboys or Confederates, Hussars,
Saxons, Romans, Japanese:

'This is where they go,' he said, gasping
Eight-year-old whom I remember then

Looking like he probably does now he's
Got a boy himself. I sat there, six.

He stood them where they stand, huge forces,
Squares and oblongs ranged along a gap, a

No-man's table, polished, with a face
Blinking off it, his, with his whole mouth a

Fogging chocolate breath. 'Now,'
He breathed, 'for the big planes, they always start it.'

I didn't disagree but was amazed
When start it was exactly what they did

And finished it in twenty seconds. 'Hugh,'
I hazarded: 'that took an hour to do.

But look at it all now.'
He did, nodding, picking out the blue

Yankees from the silver-painted Danes.
'I'll let you have one go, if you're quite sure

You've got the hang of it.' I took the hour
To set it up and of course he walked in

Saying 'Wrong, wrong, wrong, Glen,'
But picking up his planes.

We Billion Cheered

We billion cheered.
    Some threat sank in the news and disappeared.
It did because
    Currencies danced and we forgot what it was.

It rose again.
    It rose and slid towards our shore and when
It got to it,
    It laced it like a telegram. We lit

Regular fires,
    But missed it oozing along irregular wires
Towards the Smoke.
    We missed it elbowing into the harmless joke

Or dreams of our
    Loves asleep in the cots where the dolls are.
We missed it how
    You miss an o'clock passing and miss now.

We missed it where
    You miss my writing of this and I miss you there.
We missed it through
    Our eyes, lenses, screen and angle of view.

We missed it though
    It specified where it was going to go,
And when it does,
    The missing ones are ten to one to be us.

We line the shore,
    Speak of the waving dead of a waving war.
And clap a man
    For an unveiled familiar new plan.

Don't forget.
    Nothing will start that hasn't started yet.
Don't forget
    It, its friend, its foe and its opposite.

One and Another Go Home

The One flies back to his land and it dubs him King;
    the Other flies back to it too,
and glimpsed in a thicket of glancing heavies is fair
pummelled to yellow and blue and bloody good thing.

But he lives, and the sun comes up on the worked land
    lethally warm and sweet
at each a.m., and up in the loft of the future
the One and the Other meet, avert, demand,

force an agreement, a modus vivendi, a plan.
    The One shall stand for all
the hope and story of the People, the random
flame in the ancient hall and the grants of Man,

and stand for them still, still as the harvests shrink,
    and predatory neighbours
salivate on the banks, while too many children
have too many hungers, townships thrashing sink,

and the thought-out complex effort is too complex,
    too like an effort, too slow,
its answers long and slow, its questions endless,
and the One won't know, flee to or from bare facts,

be webbed as any would be in the net of how
    on earth any earth can suffer
an infinite dark increase at the rim of the meal –
while gnawing a bone the Other, remembered now,

in all four corners of counties, on all fours,
    will wait his turn until
enough are dismayed enough to muster and cry
'Whose fault is it all?' at which he goes 'Not yours.'

From the Fishermen's Bastion

It seems from here on the Bastion, on Buda,
Our backs are to the highnesses and hills
Of History, and the statuesque shadows
Stilled with all *imperial* entrails.
Those tall grey absences of the Habsburgs
Point, the point forgotten, over the Duna

At that, the capital spreading into a maze
Apparently actually endless, shimmering Pest
Beyond its riverside Parliament and the church
Szent Istvan, their two domes, the avenues east,
Rakoczy and Andrassy, diverging in such
Distance, such a lifeless, alien haze...

Between, through-voyages the brooding river,
Parting around the Margit-island, soon
Reunited south under the eyes
Of priest and saint and wed without a sound.
There goes the inkling language, Memory's:
Volga, Dnestr, Vistula, Neva, Sava,

All murmuring to the tributary hates
Both old and very old, and knowing no
Happiness that comes that way, only
Triumph, the condition of being so
Far from fatherless or collapsing lonely
By a mined road, those must needs be deserts.

For miles to the east and south and north that race
Of males who would be statues in their lives
Burn and burn their passage through the plains
As simply the simple die with their pennant loves.
Chains are busted into a thousand chains.
One struggle grows a powerful one face.

Duna's beckoning blackness as we look
Is an eye's blackness, the bars of the three bridges
Visible twinkle now while the dusk swells
And Budapest lights up like a sprinkled Christmas
As far as the eye can make it. Everywhere else
The best I know cling doggedly to the luck

That cast us on our hills and islands, rather
Than these flat scapes of unforgiving shades.
Texans, us and Germans stroll the crest;
Far Easterners snap everything that stands.
The Habsburg riders, green with edelrost,
Are floodlit. We will see them from the river.

Got Me

Far be it from me to mention
things that really happen,

but I did go to this fish farm once
and did discover this:

that despite the long cold pools of fish
outdoors and the bubbling tanks

indoors, and the rocks they sell,
(one pound fifty for a real rock)

and the age-sloughing smell of green
spawnwater and the wavering ferns,

and well, the fishes themselves –
not every mother's son is there

to make a start on a fishworld.
I mean, I made the joke –

Give me a grill pan! A joke, though.
Then I also learnt that ugly ones

are bred with selected pretty ones,
black blurting goggling ones

with ones who seem to port their orange
brains outside their orange heads

and any with the equally
slender lemon-blues.

So no wonder some don't swim as well
as I could at infant school, but

bob, and get bobbled away
by my slightest fingerdipping, don't

seem equipped even to shock,
let alone lure or blend, seem not

unlike the distressing upshot
of a baby's day of fun.

I also learnt that fish can die
of their own accord, oblivious,

and when they do they rise and float
while hell continues darting loose

below. I knew fish died! It was
seeing one side up, on the water,

length of thing with nothing in it
got me.

Sport Story of a Winner
(for Alun and Amanda Maxwell)

He was a great ambassador for the game.
                        He had a simple name.
His name was known in households other than ours.
                        But we knew other stars.
We could recall as many finalists
                        as many panellists.
But when they said this was his Waterloo,
                        we said it was ours too.

His native village claimed him as its own,
                        as did his native town,
adopted city and preferred retreat.
                        So did our own street.
When his brave back was up against the wall,
                        our televisions all
got us shouting, and that did the trick.
                        Pretty damn quick.

His colours were his secret, and his warm-up
                        raindance, and his time up
Flagfell in the Hook District, and his diet
                        of herbal ice, and his quiet
day-to-day existence, and his training,
                        and never once explaining
his secret was his secret too, and his book,
                        and what on earth he took

that meant-to-be-magic night in mid-November.
                        You must remember.
His game crumbled, he saw something somewhere.
                        He pointed over there.
The referees soothed him, had to hold things up.
                        The ribbons on the Cup
were all his colour, but the Romanoff
                        sadly tugged them off.

We saw it coming, didn't we. We knew
                    something he didn't know.
It wasn't the first time a lad was shown
                    basically bone.
Another one will come, and he'll do better.
                    I see him now – he'll set a
never-to-be-beaten time that'll last forever!
                    Won't he. Trevor.

Video Tale of a Patriot
(for David Maxwell)

START. Eton. Hice. Beaten
    in some grim urban/hopeless northern
seat. Afforded southern chances.
    Rosette. Recount. Speech. Dances.
Member. Lobbies. Froth. Committees.
    Old wife. New wife. Boards. City's.
Sir. Riches. Burgundy. Soak.
    Lord. Bypass. Bypass. Croak.

Sorry, REWIND: bypass-bypass-
    lord-soak-burgundy-riches-
sir. PLAY. 'Sir: I am increasingly
concerned at the let's say increasingly
unpredictable, unclassifiable,
    unconstructive, unreliable,
incomprehensible, reprehensible,
    a-moral, im-moral, not very sensible

acts of citizens of England of late.
    Acts not actually threatening the State
but thoroughly disconcerting. Sir:
    I saw a her who was kissing a her.
I heard the young call enemies brothers.
    I felt my money being spent on others
lying in slums, doing nothing for it.
    I smelt filth. Though I try to ignore it

it won't go away. I see vague vicars
    plastering cars with political stickers.
I read about princes visiting thieves,
    and a lord who cares what a lout believes.
I took down the numbers of those I saw
    shouting *We don't want this no more*
outside the school where a shocking percent
    appeared to have no idea what I meant,

or even what it means to be born
    a Briton. I tell you, a day will dawn
when everyone does what the blazes he wants,
    bangs his drums and performs his sundance
on what was once a proud green land,
    ruled with a disciplining spotless hand
correctly. Sir, a gent, I am sure, would
    agree with me when I –' STOP. FAST FORWARD.

The Young Ones' Nightwatch

The eight-to-twelves have got the eyes of raccoons
    what with their watching everything,
    but they're not sleeping they're learning:
    they can save their skins.

When the Slave goes to the gong and it shudders the screen
    so the Universal Planet
    spins and the blue summit
    of Paramount is seen,

they ponder and plot the star they will have to play,
    for each to be carried through
    the desperate hour or two
    to fight another day.

They shall not appear before the credits unless
    their lucky names appear
    sky-high; they shall beware
    the third name, the Guest,

or all who play a starred malevolent role
    not over quickly and when
    the dust comes down again,
    a bloody spectacle.

He's not the one, and when the heroic band
    has mustered by the flame
    for each to murmur his name
    and display his flickering hand,

they shall not be the vengeful one, the rag-bearded
    spitting one, nor charge
    infuriated, nor edge
    into the shades, rewarded

with silver and no way will they be the young
    strumming, pale and bashful
    lover, the mushy, wishful
    idealising one:

if they don't know who he is, they shall never, ever,
    under any conditions,
    pick him, fly his missions,
    trust his arriving lover.

They shall not be the third to leap the crevasse.
    They shall not flip a coin
    and win to catch a plane.
    They shall not mean yes

to the brunette pushing their arms along their backs.
    They shall not fire in anger,
    nor mock a silly danger.
    They shall know their facts.

They shall know The End is a sunset and space for two –
    some *girl* met somewhere –
    they shall not really care
    till she provides the clue

that could unlock the town to the one white horse.
    Then they shall decide.
    Righteousness and Pride
    shall ride with them of course.

They shall hit school as cool as Clint, alert
    to the Enemy, prepared,
    star-brained and hero-dared,
    ready to take and hurt,

ready for three or four reels of daylight in which
    they shall all be the One,
    all be the Strong,
    all be the Rich.

Helene and Heloise

So swim in the embassy pool in a tinkling breeze
The sisters, *mes cousines*, they are blonde-haired
    Helene and Heloise,
One for the fifth time up to the diving board,
The other, in her quiet shut-eye sidestroke
Slowly away from me though I sip and look.

From in the palace of shades, inscrutable, cool,
I watch exactly what I want to watch
    From by this swimming pool,
Helene's shimmer and moss of a costume, each
Soaking pony-tailing of the dark
And light mane of the littler one as they walk;

And the splash that bottles my whole life to today,
The spray fanning to dry on the porous sides,
    What these breathtakers say
In their, which is my, language but their words:
These are the shots the sun could fire and fires,
Is paid and drapes across the stretching years.

Now Heloise will dive, the delicate slimmer,
Calling Helene to turn who turns to see
    One disappearing swimmer
Only and nods, leans languorously away
To prop on the sides before me and cup her wet
Face before me near where I'd pictured it.

I was about to say I barely know them. –
I turn away because and hear of course
    Her push away. I see them
In my rose grotto of thought, and it's not a guess,
How they are, out of the water, out
In the International School they lie about,

What they can buy in the town, or the only quarters
Blondes can be seen alighting in, and only
    As guided shaded daughters
Into an acre of golden shop. 'Lonely?'
Who told me this had told me: 'They have no lives.
They will be children. Then they will be wives.'

Helene shrieks and is sorry – I don't think – my
Ankles cool with the splash of her sister's dive:
    I wave and smile and sigh.
Thus the happiest falling man alive,
And twenty-five, and the wetness and the brown
Hairs of my shin can agree, and I settle down.

'Already the eldest – suddenly – the problems.
The other draws, writes things.' I had heard
    Staccato horrid tantrums
Between earshot and the doorbell, held and read
Heloise's letters in chancery
Script to her dead grandmother, to me,

To nobody. They have a mother and father,
And love the largest pandas in the whole
    World of Toys. The other
Sister rang from Italy and was well,
But wouldn't come this time. 'She'll never come.
She has a home. They do not have a home.'

Stretching out in her shiny gold from the pool,
Heloise swivels, and sits and kicks
    Then reaches back to towel
Her skinny shoulders tanned in a U of lux-
Uriant material. Helene
Goes slowly to the board, and hops again

Into the dazzle and splosh and the quiet. Say,
Two, three miles from here there are heaps of what,
    Living things, decay,
The blind and inoculated dead, and a squad
Of infuriated coldly eyeing sons
Kicking the screaming oath out of anyone's.

Cauchemar. – We will be clear if of course apart,
To London again me, they to their next
        Exotic important spot,
Their chink and pace of Gloucestershire, Surrey, fixed
Into the jungles, ports or the petrol deserts.
I try but don't see another of these visits;

As I see Helene drying, Heloise dry,
The dark unavoidable servant seeming to have
        Some urgency today
And my book blank in my hands. What I can love
I love encircled, trapped and I love free.
That happens to, and happens to be, me,

But this is something else. Outside the fence,
It could – it's the opposite – be a paradise
        Peopled with innocents,
Each endowed with a light inimitable voice,
Fruit abundant, guns like dragons and giants
Disbelieved, sheer tolerance a science –

Still, I'd think of Helene, of Heloise
Moving harmless, shieldless into a dull
        And dangerous hot breeze,
With nothing but hopes to please, delight, fulfil
Some male as desperate and as foul as this is,
Who'd not hurt them for all their limited kisses.

Recollection of a Meal

She was rich in her own right.
So that either deigning to dance the slow flamenco
on any saint's day or getting her tanned arms dirty
a while at the hovering farm, she — one knew no
reason for pity really.

I got there much too early.
She showed what we could eat at the beginning,
then what we could choose at the end, and I said shyly
how very nice it all looked and this from a young
male like me isn't easy

but she looked anywhere but.
At the tall retainers and Rheinweins, at a diplomat
the black of whom was somehow a different black
from that of the lot you could make out inching back
from dull, bloodying work.

All talk was of the big bear
trapped in the heart of her ancestral forest
that very morning, early. The hussar
had seen it and was laughing, crying 'Honest!'
to them all and then to her.

Flies met on the high ceiling
over the grand dining and didn't move.
The ploy, that luring lemon pool, was ideal.
I began on the fragile squirting starter. 'In love?'
I gripped my fork. 'Well?' Ill.

'Plague?' I picked my spoon up,
glancing the eachway glance at the nodding and roaring
neighbours as long as the eye could glance, then fixed
both eyes on the plate and shells and name, daring
a trembling hand and one sip

of a hot notorious best
below its guiltless foam. That made me a starman,
instantly and confidently modest,
sharing my experience, my mouthful charm, and
settling in as a hinting guest

to the acceleration
of the meal – a dab, the slick hands coloured orange
easing the picked-at plates away, the aimless
flirt with the diagonally-across-from-me angel,
my falling, filling wineglass,

the arriving topped desserts,
bries and dolcelattas, unsealed, bulging.
But my grand exit, to the sea-green marble *Gents*
where ambassadors sighed and punned in the pungent
echoey air, was my chance –

to wait for her own polite
exit to where she'd have to go, via where
I stood, and then to comment, and to light
her cigarillo, and not seem to care
even as she'd hurry by

and on into the yellow
alabaster *Ladies*! Would you credit
she never came? Too rich to be so empty,
surely to God, she was rich in her own right,
but no, she never met me

again and I doggedly made
sure of that: when the minks filled and collected
outside the cloakroom, I was calm and hid,
and when the glassy table clearly reflected
her face, I was under it

amusing the gathered cats.
They did for the fallen food while we all waited
for her to swish out. It's a piece of piss to look back
and label it, like 'fin de siècle' – admit it,
we are gods at retrospect –

but did she deserve what came?
You'll say: 'She never deserved what she had.' Okay,
I'll say the same. Okay. And anyway, I'm
now remembering faces on that Sunday,
straw-sucking, open, dumb,

marooned by the shut gates.
And I wasn't awfully well, and the so-rich food.
And she was only so beautiful. And those cats
they did look peckish, and the diplomats were rude
as graffiti. One forgets.

Although, when one enjoys and
is eating during an era, one scarcely thinks
of the next one, does one? Think what would have happened!
She'd have to have stripped the ladies of the minks,
opened the french windows

for the day workers, freed
those flies, then let the sad grizzly's ankle
out of its clotting ring, then disagreed
in different ways with every banker's angle,
then understood what the dead

were on about. Equally,
I'd have to have jumped her by the door for *Dames*,
hooded her, pulled her, thrown her in the back of my
2CV and motored to kingdom come,
telling her why on the way.

Rare Chat with the Red Squirrel

No even now, when your
once astonished, once muttering, once
blurting, lastly listening faces group
and grey in a demi-circle in this home garden,
I can surprise you.

Not with my rare colour,
– you protest at 'rare', you who had, yes you,
pinned me down on your recto 'Extinct in England',
and you who scribbled 'hoax' when you even saw me,
manning the riddled elm,

or after, at my capture,
sniffed round me like a wine-sharp, or a
buyer about to nudge his honey and show her
'you see this is painted on' – but even then
you wouldn't have it:

you merely substituted
'common' then, like it made you less the wrongdoer,
envisaging squads of us and I the ringleader
swiftly nailed. You wouldn't believe a murmur
on my bushy red honour.

Nor when the grey,
fresh from his walnut elevenses,
bared his teeth at the bars till the cops inferred
yes, I was that victim and made me feel so
strangely guilty

as he was handled away,
and I said 'You dig, that wasn't the actual grey
who did my nutkin over – he was another,
and I'd know his red eyes anywhere, 'cause
hell, I'm in them', no,

you caged me again,
and locked and stood and pondered what I did.
It was sodding dark in there with my surname's red
uncaught by light, so nothing. I cocked my head
for one measly eureka

but the way it went was, like,
a burning bath to see if my red would leak,
an X-ray into what was making me talk,
a bastard prod to see what made me not talk,
a mugshot, an APB –

fine, fine way to love me.
But gentlemen, ladies, that is the better-left-
unsaid past you notice I always say.
You would too, but let us enjoy this day.
Everybody looks grey

who waits in the oaks
and ashes for that time when with my eyes
hurt on a text, and nuts beside my nut-tray,
Nature takes her run-up and I'm quick with love
but not quick enough, so,

in the long mean time,
listen only to how the noise you hear
in your wide language differs in no respect
from what you heard when I first happened on nut,
or burst from the grey horde

who got the rest, for I know
you listen to me not for a new wisdom,
nor music nor aloneness in my England,
and nor for what remains of my red coat,
nor that you thought me dead,

though that perturbed you
maybe a little, no? You know it's only
my bound, hic and squeak when I rub my eyes.
Beats me why, cross my heart, but it's a song
you should recognise.

Out of the Rain

I

The animals went in two by two, but I,
alive elsewhere, had been in the loudest town,

pleading. How do I start to explain to you
what was lost, and how, and even before

the rain that came and came?
Yes, it was fun in town. We've never denied

the length of the silver dresses, the babble and haze
of Friday nights and hell, even Sunday nights,

yes. I'd go into detail but I myself
was bright with it all and tended to misting over

if you see what I mean. My Ex was still around
then, but she wouldn't vouch for this, even if

she'd made into the line herself, and she hadn't.
I hadn't either, and this – this is that story.

II

I do remember the last of the hottest days,
because Brack and I were picked to play for the Jungle.

He scored six and I was awarded the red.
Some of those lofty brothers played for the Town,

while their daddy hammered his embarrassing huge boat
on a day like that! The crowd would watch our match

then turn and laugh at the noise from the harbour. Ha!
Some of their people were out like that, in fact,

couldn't concentrate, and finally
conceded they couldn't win. Gallid walked

tensely to the platform for his shot,
and split the green to a three'er, and in a suit!

We linked our bats and danced to the Winners Bar,
anxious for tall foaming Manzadinkas!

III

I know what you think: that meanwhile He held a trial
of thunderclouds and picked one blacker than black,

and patted its hair and said 'Go On, boy, Go Back
And Bring 'Em Hell!' but no, it was just our luck.

– The Weatherman, anyway, had said
the hot spell wouldn't hold, and of course why should it?

He showed us the LOWs, poised at the edge of the world,
the Weatherman, and he grinned and said 'Good night.'

Then they showed our match! They did a feature
on Gallid, what an old star he was, and they say

they showed Brack and I, falling around on the lawn
some time after eleven. Lucky they did,

really, because we don't remember a thing.
We were out of our little skulls, in the jungle.

IV

Before I finally – hell, and it's been a while –
tell about then, the end of the last dry night,

it's worth remembering what had been going on.
We'd had a shit-hot summer, that's for sure,

and the office guys were free to roll their sleeves
and booze or participate, or both, and did.

There was a song that stayed top of the charts,
wouldn't fucking budge. It was called *I*

Want It Now – interesting thing about that:
they told me the tough little singer was last seen nude

and paddling through the studio, I mean really,
great video, or what? But her band were drowned.

What else – the Town won every bloody game
up to that day. I'm kind of proud of that.

V

The animals. Big question, yes, of course:
How did the son-of-a-prophesying-bitch

find them all? – what's the word – the logistics.
Answer: haven't a clue. We did see lorries

parked on the slip road. There was that night with Coops
and my Ex, she was also Coops's Ex, creeping

up to the lorries and banging them and hearing
nothing. I mean, the hollow bong. So we thought

these had been left behind by some small firm
suddenly gone to hell. So we went home.

In retrospect they must have been full of insects.
And there were the quiet trains.

Haggit's kid kept saying in the morning
'There are trains going by and nobody hears them!'

VI

You're starting to think: morons. But what was suspicious?
We assumed they were fuel trains, the secret ones,

and we weren't about to sully our hands with politics.
Anarchists, we weren't. Arseholes maybe.

But I haven't forgotten the buses.
Green, beige, pink and blue buses,

obsolete, used in the tourist season.
We thought – who wouldn't – the old crock was cashing in

like everybody else. I mean, old Haggit,
bless his last words ('You'll drown') was by that time

selling water, and Coops's surgery
was pay-as-you-enter, pay-as-you-stitch, and I

was preaching at a very slight profit.
All we thought was that he was doing what we were.

VII

I'm trying to read the diaries I had
but it's all smudged, and I have to hum that song

to haul it back. Then there's a certain smell
fumes up that summer like nothing else on earth...

– Burning green leaves, his trees dying the death.
They tried to pass a law, you know, to stop him,

pretending they gave a toss about his woodland
when all they wanted to do was show him he couldn't

do what he wanted any more, because.
Because it was unnerving them, in the heat.

Because they didn't know why he was doing it.
Because, because. Because he was doing it.

They rushed it through. The Council hurried to stop
this outrage, as the last tree was lopped.

VIII

I suppose it's still on the statute-book in some
soaking hell. Where was I? In the jungle,

after the match. There was, I remember now,
a last-night-of-the-show feel to it all,

which I'd know about, as I was no slouch on the stage
either, and our production of *Gomorrah*

was banned at once and played to shrieking houses!
Me, I played the lawyer, my lines were

'Shut up, I don't need to know' and 'No you can't'
and – can't remember, something about a warrant.

Coops was a headless king, my Ex his widow,
and Haggit played himself but not very well.

Good days. But yes, it did feel a bit, you know,
like, what the hell would there be to do tomorrow?

IX

In the Winners Bar there'd been Olde Tyme Oyle,
there'd been Manzadinka by the gallon, Chuice,

Diet Light, pints and pints of Splash,
and all the usual girls between the curtains.

There'd been songs of winning, anthems of the Jungle
Club, there'd been speeches and falling down,

and taunts and chants directed at the Town!
I mean it was quite a night, and I've asked myself:

what the hell did we head to the jungle for?
There was Brack and I, Haggit, the blue winger,

the mascot with his mushrooms, and some girl.
We'd most of us played for the Jungle, but so what?

It didn't mean we came from there, although
the winger did – and that girl, and in fact the mascot.

X

Funny how all in the space of what was maybe
half an hour, everything that was starting

clearly announced it was starting. There was a rumble.
There was a vast boomerang of birds

black against the black-green of the jungle's
drenched sky: there was a second, different rumble.

We had a debate. We were always having debates.
Even out of our tiny heads, we were picking

fair sides to wonder what the hell
the rumbles were, and how far away they were.

The junglies – Brack was calling them that
and right to their little faces – the junglies all

got nervous. The winger, who'd not touched a drop, was sure
the war was starting – 'Or at least two different wars!'

XI

The girl, who'd arrived with somebody nobody knew
and had lost him, or just left him with his drink,

made to speak, but so did Haggit. Then
the girl said 'N-n-no, it's a great

elephant larger than any town!' The mascot
gulped and seconded that, but said it was green.

Then Haggit scoffed, and Brack said, 'That's no elephant,'
as a third rumble came, 'That's my mother!'

And so it was left to me to feel the cold,
and calm them down. 'Sod it, it's just thunder.'

Full marks for irony, of course, but remember,
it had been a good nine months. Then Haggit and Brack

got serious and agreed. Which meant the junglies
were outvoted, as the girl had disappeared.

XII

More obviousnesses then. Sheet lightning.
God's face in it, bored, on His chin.

One of us shouting, 'Knock if off!' to Him.
And suddenly it stopping, at our shins.

'Ahem, let's go home,' ventured Haggit,
wobbling on a log. 'We'll get a chill.'

And we asked the blue winger, who in our game
had played what they call a blinder, to help out

for teammates' sakes, by showing us our way.
Brack was getting jumpy. 'What do you say?

Will you help us out, us three?'
It was very dark. He was speaking to a tree.

'Fucking fairweather friend,' he spat. 'Blue freak!'
And the mascot giggled and we were up shit creek.

XIII

No wonder Brack was losing it: after all,
he was a news-hound, that was what he did.

They'd be screeching for him, threatening his friends
back in the newsroom – 'Where's Brack? IT RAINED!'

He could hardly call in sick, after his great
heroics in the match, and his face in the News:

so he knew he was out of a job.
No of course he didn't know we all were.

Haggit, meanwhile, he had a wife and kid,
who'd certainly be waiting to be angry.

But he was a calm kind of a man, and he said
'Let's work it out from the light.' I said 'What light?'

I do admit I was hardly a help. I kept thinking
of the losers happy in the Winners Bar, drinking.

XIV

We waded where we thought we'd waded from.
We couldn't lose the mascot, who kept saying

'Whistlework, whistlework,' and our only
guide was the one cloud pierced

by the moon, and only at times.
Otherwise it was dark and the only sounds

were the mascot and, ultimately, Brack
drowning it. Then we were worried men

and cold, thinking of lawns and admitting it.
We waded on, it got drier, higher up,

a good sign, for our port was on a hill.
That's why they called us mad, but we didn't choose

to have the sea up there, where the ancient bloke
had made his boat, and we called him mad too.

XV

They called us – not only mad – wait for it,
the Golden Generation. It was our cars,

and our carefree times, our drinks on the roofs of homes,
our tilted velvet hats in the winter, our games

and how we used our leisure, made it work for us,
our softness on ourselves, our relaxed

attitude to money. Most of all,
because we called ourselves Golden. And hell,

good times. But as I say – that last night air:
what would there be to do tomorrow? More.

More of the gazing over the black-tiled floor
for that single someone, more of the same jazz

in all four corners of the cars, and more
seasons of the League, and those hot days.

XVI

We were near the shore. We knew that by the smell
of salt and gull, and sometimes the sound

of breakers but Haggit shrugged and said 'Thunder.'
I didn't think so. Brack

seemed to snag his ankle on each tree
like he was trying to, and the moon came right

out, and we caught each other's eyes. 'Right,'
said Brack: 'this is a nightmare. Pinch my cheek.'

I closed my eyes, while Haggit lost his temper,
and so it was I who heard them – girls' voices.

Drunk as us, drunker than us, moving
towards us not away from us, and many:

Brack said 'This is a dream. Leave me alone.'
Haggit and I just stood. We were shaking.

XVII

A second's realisation of torchlight.
A second second's seeing we were found...

'Hoo, trolls! Look who's been in the rain!
Ahoo, aha! A treasury of wet men!'

'Is it really them?' 'Is it really who?' 'No!
It isn't them, it's men!' 'Where was the party,

and what were you?' There were six or seven of them,
they had cloaks, they were on their way from something, I

actually thought I knew a couple. Anyway,
they were townspeople all right, and I breathed again.

Brack was talking about our match, our win,
and our looking for fun, but Haggit was squatting down

a misery in the water. One girl said
'Did you hear the wars? Did you hear the elephants?'

XVIII

The wind blew. Another girl said this:
'We're swimming out to the Island for tonight!

There's your fun, heroes! Nobody's there
at this time, and we've got some hammocks there

and Manzadinka, yay! out on the Island,
and then in the morning we swim home to sleep.'

I'm not telling you this because they all
died out there – of course they did, they woke

and there wasn't land – I'm telling you why
it sounded such fun, and why Brack said 'Come on!'

and went with them. It's not like he was mad
or irresponsible, I mean, he was,

but he'd lost his job by then, and he had no kids
or wives to speak of. I had to stay with Haggit.

50

XIX

Then there's a blank time –
Haggit had stopped talking, or when he did

he was talking to Brack, and I said 'He isn't there'
but it's very vague, though I do remember the girls

in their blowing firelight, trying to lure us
into the woods to change our minds, then suddenly

running away in silence. Then the wind
colossal in the trees, and drops again.

All those trees, all those millions of trees.
Could've come in handy. Wish I'd been

elected, in on it, if you know what I mean –
rather than what I was, the last to make it

out of the sea, the miracle in wet clothes.
Swearing oaths.

XX

The animals went in two by two, I saw them –
later, later, after the girls and the lightning

illuminating the black ocean and figures
swimming out to their shrinking island, after

the still mascot, and after the rain resuming,
and the last dry inch of my body, and Haggit's

wild decision to climb to the top of a pine:
'What are you doing? Come down, come down, come down!' 'I'm

staying here till it's over, son. I can see
hundreds of clouds coming. I don't see the town.

Stay on the earth if you have to, but you'll drown!'
'I won't!' 'You will!' 'I won't!' Well I won't rub it in,

but when the wall of water broke the spit
it would have swamped those pines in about a minute –

XXI

but after I started to run, later, I saw them:
I must have been some way inland,

where the country rose again and rather than wading
I splashed through groves and glades – but it was

amazing – a dry risen corridor of light
guarded (I crouched and shook) through which in, yes,

yawn, yawn, in pairs, the animals went,
some still sleeping, some complaining,

one or two reading, others crying,
others terrified by the mauve heavens

or pointing out God to friends who knew it was Him,
I mean who else would show Himself at a time

like this? But it was just a cloud
and it split in half.

XXII

I backed away, and the light drummed on my back
as I ran and ran and just as I decided

to say a prayer before I died, I tripped
and collided with a stone – or with a square.

I had a square in my mind when I blacked out,
and a square in front of me when I was choked

awake by the water rising. It was a garden
path stone, the first of thirty stones

zigzagging up to a door where a Unicorn
asked me the last animals I saw.

'I saw two Zebras. Following two Yaks.'
'What's your name?' the Unicorn wondered.

I gave it. 'Ah, then you missed your place in the queue.
Like us. But we were always going to.'

XXIII

And these in my dazed state were only words,
though you see they stuck. I blinked, and felt

my whole frame lifted on to a warmth
of animal, white, white animal,

– did I say Unicorn? Yes,
a Unicorn, and it was bearing me

out of the rain, into a room of lamps
and beating lives all blurring into a focus.

They were all animals I hadn't seen,
and never did again, though I saw them now.

They all resembled what I knew, but either
thinner, gentler, slower, or a new colour

and I sat in a ring with them whatever they were,
and the Unicorn sat opposite, and said these words...

XXIV

'One day they came and took the Cat, who'd lied.
They left behind the Other, who'd said nothing.

They came again, and took the eating Dog,
while the Other stopped and offered his food, and stared.

They came again, and fooled the Elephant
who wanted to be fooled; the Other didn't.

They took the Fox next, who seemed reluctant,
and told the Other "You stay here on watch."

They took the Jackdaw who was screaming "I!"
which left the Other, quiet, making a nest.

No problem for the righteous Lion: he went,
but the Other was troubled, needed time to think.

When they next came, the Monkey had packed a case,
but the Other, puzzled, had nothing to put in a case.

XXV

Then the Natterjack, told he'd meet a Princess,
leapt in the air, but the Other fell about.

The Owl put down his book, said "I deserve",
and told the Other "I find you don't deserve."

The Pig – you should have seen him – he almost flew!
But the Other couldn't, so wouldn't, but still hopes to.

The Shark was next – and you know this trip was free?
– he paid a million; the Other said "Not me."

The Sheep were hard to separate, but one
went with the ones who went, and the Other stayed

with the ones who stayed. The Snake was next, accusing
the Other so silently he never knew

why he was left behind with the likes of me
and the Other Unicorn, who stayed with me.'

XXVI

And who then came in with towels, which reminded me:
'Why one at a time? I saw double that.'

Which made her laugh. 'We saw you on the news,
we know about your escapades! – but listen:

are you just a drunken Man – or part of the business?
Who were the ones who went?' 'Nobody went

anywhere!' I cried, 'It was just raining!
There'll be a hell of a lot of mud in the morning!

– but nobody died, did they? What are you saying?'
'Oh,' said a huge bird sadly,

'has anyone been doing something odd
recently, in your town? Like, building something?'

'Only the man with the trees, this local twit,
building a sort of – big...oh shit.'

XXVII

I suppose I overreacted. The lines were down
anyway, and the lights were packing in.

They put me to bed a while, which I shared with something
not unlike a Woman, but comprehensible

and with one face. I couldn't sleep. The rain
never let up, and I went downstairs again.

Some of the furrier guests were thinking of
turning in by then, but things like bats,

otters, hedgehogs – brighter colours, though –
began to reminisce, just wouldn't go,

and the mousy thing in the coat just stared and stared
out of the window.

I ended the night at chess with the bored Yeti.
'Did your companion go?' I asked. 'Dunno.'

XXVIII

I must have got my second wind then,
as the next thing I remember is a full

harmonious hum of snoring, in the dark,
ranging from the unhearable to the zurr

of a bearish group in the library, and always
the rain and as I left,

as I stood on the WELCOME mat and said my quiet
'So long' to the left behind, left them,

and ventured out to the light and the first stone,
I saw an extraordinary thing, – I mean,

even by these standards – how the whole
garden and cottage, seething with the asleep,

was a deep deep hole in the sea, and all around
the walls of water poured against the ground!

XXIX

Nobody was disturbed but I – I saw
water, white with fury at this Law,

fall and fountain again, against its will,
leaving us dry and pocketed, a well

of oxygen in what was the end of a world.
The greenness here, the life of it, was so strong

I thought 'Nobody's wrong, nothing's wrong'
and it felt like my first thought, and I felt how the grass

stayed bone dry to the last.
I thought of waking the Unicorns, and just as I

thought to myself 'There are no such things
as unicorns' the water spurted out

and gripped my feet and whirled me up this spout
and onto the flat sea and that was that.

XXX

Day, I guess. The sky was a sagging grey.
Everywhere dead land and debris,

and after swimming in turn to three of the four
horizons of the dome,

I twisted to look at the last, and it had to be home.
Home, though it shouldn't have been, was a high

ridge with its back to the sea,
and the rain would have to have filled the valley before

the town would flood, although by then
it would have done, and had.

So what were left were the roofs, and the high arena
where we did our plays, and also the Heroes Tower

which from these miles seemed swollen at its steeple
like a hornets' nest on a stick. Clinging people.

XXXI

I swam, and thought of the dead. I thought 'They're dead.'
(I was known as a thinker at school, I'll have you know.)

I thought of the things I'd seen, and thought 'I didn't
see those things.' (I was known as a liar, too.)

I swam over trees and everything I had once
run through, and it all seemed much simpler

and, feeling my confidence build, I stood on the water,
which didn't take my weight. I sank, I swam.

It began to rain again, and had always rained.
I imagined the Winners Bar an aquarium.

Which made me think of the match, which led to the thought
of the noise of the hammering father in his harbour,

which led me to scan the horizon
for his boat and zoo, but no, they were gone like him −

XXXII

− to the Dry, the Saved, the Impossibly Full: a book.
Good end for all that wood, I thought, blankly.

Then I caught some floating door
and lay on it, closed my eyes and trusted it:

we would float upsea to the town.
And we floated upsea to the town.

What was left of it, well yes, we've all seen pictures,
but it's really only another view, only

the dead are about and prices have fallen down,
there's no sport played for a while, and the Police

are pally or warn and fire. Charities come,
and interviewers and the place becomes

famous. But − hell, famous for whom?
Well, okay. Nobody this time.

XXXIII

Washed in, I was reckoned dead. When I woke again
I was on dry land on a roof with the whole Council.

In fact I disturbed a debate on the recent crisis
and the Mayor, about to cast his casting vote,

nulled and voided the meeting. All my fault.
They adjourned to look at the view, and as I crawled

and stumbled back to an upright position, an old
stalwart took me aside and told me 'Oh,

what a great debate it was!
Some insist we're afloat on a floating detached

roof, others that this is the one building
left, i.e. we've been chosen above all

not to, er, and so on.' 'How did you vote?'
'Oh come on, secret ballot, sir, and all that.'

XXXIV

And then I saw all eyes were on me, the one
neither dead, nor drowning, nor on the Council.

So I said 'Here you are – where are the real people?'
A hushed hiatus then, but the Mayor said 'There,

there', and I told him to stuff his sympathy,
but he pointed at where the Tower had been and where

it now was, a rolling log that couldn't
help any of the hundreds trying to grip it

and splashing to matey death, in each other's way.
The Mayor sat down with me,

and they say I suddenly lost it and screamed at him
to go to the house in the wood and help them in,

and find the lot in the boat and scuttle them!
The Mayor looked at his watch: 'Gentlemen,

XXXV

Time is immaterial. We have
a roof, we have about two dozen men,

we have the bust of the founder, which is round...
I reckon that just about makes a troppling ground!'

And so they played, and I looked out to the sea,
and the sea and the dead, the drowning, the dead and the sea,

and then I joined in a while and managed a five-o
before losing out to the Mace-Man's cunning yellow.

'Ha! Not looking, were you?' the Mace-Man roared,
as the rain from heaven pissed on our troppling board.

'It's slackening off', a fielder said. He seemed
curiously blue for a town official,

but hell he was right about that, and the Weatherman stared
up at the sky, and said 'I want to bat.'

XXXVI

By the time we reached half-time the air was only
dirty, a muzzy brown, like a sand but nothing.

The rain was hardly rain, more like a reminder.
The level remained level. The sea was headless.

We were winning 16-9 with a red in the bucket.
I was always, always going to say 'Oh, fuck it'

as I walked and dived and swam and looked back only
to see a half-mile away

the prizes passing from Mayor to Man, and the caps
thrown in the air and to hear,

small on the wind like the smell of men, 'hooray!'
and then a silence, then

'hooray', tinier than can be, and then
'hooray', and silence. Nothing. This is me.

XXXVII

I was born where I knew no man, nor that
the rain would fall, nor end, nor that a boat

would sail away and none that I knew would follow.
All that I knew are gone, and all

that I know I love and is here and knows it will not
know me tomorrow.

I was born, I know, in a town which never
should have been built where it was, but was,

and I live in this same one next to the sea
where nothing changes but is.

But is that one cloud ever going
to move again, as I bat and believe

it will, or is that the sentence passed?
Time has gone, townspeople, townspeople, time is lost.

XXXVIII

I've been working on this page,
for an age, in the sun.

I'll move towards the open window,
place my hands in the sun.

I'll stroll out to the match where we are
winning it in the sun.

We are two points clear in every league there is.
Bar none.

I'll stroll back from the match where we are
coasting home in the sun.

I'll see my Ex through the open window or
someone, tanned in the sun.

We'll love and laugh and win at all we do.
Or have done.

XXXIX

'Yes, well I'm an authority on history',
I tell the eight Reserves when I meet them

in the Winners Bar, taking the daily pictures
of one of only how many survivors?

they ask me, but I shake my head: 'No questions!'
They think I'm joking and they shake my hand.

I give a boy an autograph. I gave him it
yesterday. I'll give him it tomorrow.

I wonder what he thinks of me. The Weatherman
goes past. He's out of a job. I say I'm sorry.

Two of the Council, Gingham and Sub-Gingham,
always mention unicorns when they pass me.

They think that's funny. Gennit, the matchwinner,
shuts them up with a look. And goes past me.

XL

Guess what I saw. 'Your Ex? and she was standing
out on the pitch and waving, wearing a silk

she cut with your own money? and she so wanted
you to go up, so you did,

and she spoke in a new way and her silk came down
and all that was there was yours and you married in town!

Am I right? Oh I'm sorry.
What did you see?' Forget it. Don't worry.

The game is starting now, anyway.
Shall we go and see that game? If we win

we'll be two points clear. So I hope we win. If we win
let's go to the Winners Bar, I've a seat there. 'Yeah?

What's your poison?' Manzadinka.
Manzadinka! 'What?' Manzadinka!

XLI

I can see you through this glass,
all of you. Go on, guess, guess,

guess what I saw. No, a weather forecast.
I'm telling you the truth. It was illegal

but they let it happen. 'Oh.' Is that what you say?
Oh? Yes, I overheard it happen.

'And.' Is that what you say?
And? Is that all? Well. And nothing.

Still the same. Yes, you're dead right I'm mad.
I could see you through the glass, you had a horn

and so did he, you were making fun of me.
But tell them, Mr Councillor, who scored

the Double-Green that day, when the Town were out
for two pinks and a fifty – tell them that!

XLII

I wake in a hot morning, and I make
a breakfast for a man who needs a breakfast!

Nothing has changed. I warm the last night coffee
and reread the local paper, where it says

we won and we are two points clear. The sun
is high above my home. Nothing has moved.

We're favourites for the match today. But don't think
for a moment we won't try.

I hope my Ex will phone. I mow the lawn.
I lecture. I once saw a unicorn.

No, two. I turn my personal radio on.
I Want It Now has gone to Number One.

I finish this and put it on the shelf.
I take it down and send it to myself.

II. LOOK A RAINBOW

Dream but a Door

Dream but a door slams then.
Your waking is in the past. The friend
who left was the last to leave and that
left you, calm as a man.

Wash in a slip of soap belonging
only a week ago to a girl but
yours now and washed to a nothing.
As you and she, friends and not.

Eat to the end as toast,
the loaf she decided on, only last
Saturday last. The crust is what
you said you'd have. So have.

Stop by the calender, though,
and peel. The colour today
is yellow, and you will never remember
what that means – 'J'.

Drink to the deep the coffee, down
to the well of the dark blue cup.
The oaf with the nose of steam is alive
and well again. Look up.

Grown and Who Means

Jacketed and British among the bare
Fresh of neither in light on Commonwealth Ave.,
I glimpse what thickening jaw and wild hair
You – and I call him you now – worry and have.

We did come here before, in the sun before.
We didn't come here, I order and am alone.
– No dad or kid is made to feel sympathy for
Whom merely feels grown and who means grown

Not in the washed-out sense of my red eyes close
Sooner than, or I wrinkle with how to cross
Advancing desert hours in this skin, or those
I giggled with are a husband or a boss,

But *grown*, passively flowering in a light
Before some alien and considering sight.

That Evening That

How lonely it gets,
as the dream, having come to pass,
remains a dream as well as like a dream.

And somebody will come, eating,
hoping, – though to think,
however long and vague that meal,
superb the sex, same and varied, how-
ever rose that evening,

that nobody will ever be
here, where everybody is, is
if no consolation,
fascinating as that will be,
and fascinating as that this sound

is silence,
that this is the past,
and that I who love you am not beside you.

Desire of the Blossom

This strain bloomed red. It became tended:
Admirable, colourful, a flower
In the good corner. No more green wildfire
Threatening no promising: that
    Pollen-coaxing
Act had ended.

And eyes had me, noses neared and dwindled.
Cameras' mutated insect heads.
Partakers came to tag all sorts of reds
They marked in me: Royal Mail Red,
    Robin and Blood-Red,
Vigil Candle,

Ibis, Ripper, Cardinal and Crab-
Apple. Then they went and I remain
This pleased awhile, in a glow – sane,
Boiling with their help, cooled
    Fitfully by the night
And the dew-web

Nagging me woken, wired, sustained – red.
But say, of a morning, may I, (dreamt I), one
Morning shake like an animal in rain
These ribbons off and look
    A neglected species
The colour Mud?

Cause if, I would remove to a far garden,
Cold, unphotogenic, dry to the sight,
Proffering no petal, no respite
From strict time, then ugly,
    Vegetable, fibrous,
Strain and harden.

19/9/91

The leaves usher in this:
the unromantic yes
of the unpersuaded girl
by the blue, smoky wall at the start of term.

Term must have begun
by now, by how the town
is pale, sniffing, cold
with hurt mothers, the elderly and me here.

This is the year's click.
The 0.0 of the clock.
Now for the hope and date
again and the foggy walk, the light in windows!

– As if I had met myself,
swallowed and set off
in two directions: down,
chuckling as I deepen on towards Christmas,

and up, expecting yes,
experience getting less,
with something still to ask
of somebody at a desk in the high summer.

The Beast and Beauty

1. *The Beast and Time*

Here on this my overgrown and empty
Echoing estate, Time has become
The gooseberry with no plans to leave,
Thanks to a chuckling curiosity:
    Will the barefoot, the silver-laugh
        Leave home

For this, for the Great Lawn and Ancient Wing,
The flagstones of the Courtyard I alone
Clank across, vanishing into the misty
Orchard, for the dew on the old swing,
    The joy-to-see brave the dusty
        Domain

Of this my peering, spot-in-a-window face?
Time remains at the piano and wants to know.
When day is ending, smoky, pink and dry,
He puts on lights in every wing. But he's
    No right to hang on here and I
        Say so.

2. *The Beast Alone*

Beauty don't come today.
I have a walk to take, an elm to fell.
I meant to do it some time this year
The seventh since you went but what the hell,
It's about time I got it seen to, eh?
So not today, my dear.

And not tomorrow either.
One of the fat white pigeons means to sing
And you wouldn't expect another beast to miss it,
Would you? And there's still the bell to ring
In celebration of the warmer weather,
And the snow's soft visit.

Rushed off my feet, I am,
What with the walking across the carpet reading,
The staring at the sundial, and the grounds.
All of this would bore you, and the weeding
Tire you out. And plus you'd have to come
To help me beat the bounds.

Better not be this year.
You wouldn't want this great deserted pile
To fall apart for lack of care now, would you?
If you did come, you'd have to search a while
Anyway, to find me working here.
So look hard, won't you.

3. *Beast's Good Dream*

It's dark in all particulars but souls
(The word comes bringing souls) are blown like kites
        Or swimming to and fro;
Images smear off them as they go
As if too fast for eyes, let alone thoughts,
        They go down holes,
Or faces loop about in strings of noughts.

Here, wherever it is but it is here,
The generous grandpa comes as a small girl
        Determined to be kind,
Succeeds in that and spins; you blink and find
A former lover surly as a troll
        And turning male with fear;
A rogueish uncle as a weeping doll,

Your decent sisters gentlemen in green,
And your true friends a family at tea.
        An irritant at your ear
You swat to a millionth death and then you hear
It fall three octaves into the everyday
        Expert on the screen
And waddle, tilted, boring, on its way.

Suspended, you remember you can see
In seven ways and see, where all is tones
        Of violet, red, brown,
A figure waltzing solo, staring down
At many feet and through the dazzling panes
        At an amazing sea.
But when you look again it's dark and rains

And a bully shuffles by, shielding her toy.
Most in fact are children, few have time
        To catch the breath they want;
They burst across your path and point and pant
And go somewhere. A boy burbles a name
        And jumps into a boy
Who jumps into a boy who does the same.

Bluer, later on, you swear you saw
The only thing of white and next you do,
        It makes a Y of light,
And neither turns nor twists but rises right
Towards where you remain: its face is new,
        Or never known before,
You know it's beautiful but think it's you:

It isn't; what it is – and then you wake
And thread your song through all the dusty hours –
        Is someone you have met,
One you have forgotten, will forget
But ultimately know. The image blurs;
        You do not age, you ache.
Elsewhere a bedsheet never stirs, then stirs.

4. *The Beast to Beauty*

I know how long it's been, Beauty, alone.
I know by how the orchard's overgrown,
By generations of increasingly
Multi-coloured starlings, and by me.
Not by my face, which stays Beast's one face,
But by the dated scraps around this place
Everywhere, the mornings blowing about.
I know by my great vintages running out.

I know, moreover, how much time remains
Before the unlikely footfall, sudden, tense,
Across the markless gravel, and the knock,
Unearthliness of luck staring at luck,
And you approaching and approaching now.
Beauty, I know all this, though hardly how.

Plaint of the Elder Princes

We are the first and second sons of kings.
We do the most incredibly stupid things.
 When we meet Elves
 We piss ourselves;
When we see adults walking around with wings,

We crack up laughing and we take the mick.
We wind up in a cloud or we get sick,
 Or turned to stone,
 Or wedding a crone
And running widdershins and damned quick,

Or otherwise engaged, up to our eyes.
We brag, we stir, we mock and we tell lies.
 Upon our Quest
 Eight Kingdoms west
We find no peace: nobody evil dies.

No, seven Witches have a Ball and go to it.
Our sweethearts meet a toad and say hello to it.
 We bet it's our
 Brother De-ar:
It is, we ask a favour, he says no to it.

We are the first and second sons of Queens.
We have our chances and our crucial scenes
 But it comes up Tails
 While Our Kid scales
The castle walls with some wild strain of beans

To make his dream come out. What about ours?
We've wished on every one of the lucky stars:
 Got on with Wizards
 And off with Lizards,
Sung the gobbledegook to Arabian jars,

But no: we serve to do the right thing wrong,
Or do the bad thing first, or stagger along
 Until it's time
 For the Grand Old Rhyme
To drop and make our suffering its song.

The Fool implied that we were 'necessary'
In his last lay. This made us angry, very.
   Perhaps we are,
   But his guitar
Has found a lodging quite unsanitary.

'Typical Them!' we hear them say at court:
'Brutal, selfish, arrogant, ill-taught!'
   They thought we would
   Turn out no good
And lo! we turned out just as they all thought,

We first and second Princes of the Blood.
Dreaming of a woman in wood.
   Scaring the birds,
   Lost for words,
Weeds proliferating where we stood;

But hell, we have each other, and the beer.
Our good-for-nothing pals still gather here
   To booze and trample
   And set an example
From which the Golden Boy can bravely veer.

We're up, and it's a fine day in the land.
Apparently some Princess needs a hand.
   It's us she wants?
   Okay. This once.
Show us the map. This time we'll understand.

Tale of Robbing Wood

When what the hell was written on the sky
'Oh look at this' said Hobden looking down
At the page spread of print: 'this Robbing Wood
    He's at it again, he found
Our finest quartering a doe and said
Or – so it says down here – *demanded* why!'

'Why' monotoned his woman, knitting a woman:
'Why' 'Why indeed!' spluttered her rising lord:
'Presumably he believes he's in his rights
    To strut about the wood –
It's in his name! Wood! yes? – picking fights
With noble – noblemen. Outrageous! Someone

Should put a stop to this!' 'Yes,' said his wife,
'Why were they quartering a doe, I mean.'
'Wh–? Wh–? Wh–?' And a slamming door,
    And then, on the village green
That afternoon a kind of council of war
With the mercer, the fletcher, the chandler and chief

Crier: 'Master Hobden, it don't stop there!
I heard he knobbled the County Hunt last week!
Just him and this clergyman he stuck the fox
    Right up his tussock! The cheek!'
'It can't go on,' said the manufacturer of clocks,
Walking towards them carrying a chair.

The fletcher whispered 'they say he is actually green.
Comes from a green tribe, sort of, they wants
To do us all in but first them in the north.
    I heard this at the wantz.'
They looked at him. 'But what about us down south,
When are we?' one called from his demesne.

Later they had some other names: Skillet,
Jonson, Tuck, and soon some news to swallow
Somehow: Wood had disturbed an entire chapter
    Of noblemen in a hollow
Having their way with the digenous pop. 'He stopped a
Sheriff – would you please – and a whole billet

Of lads like mine were holed up in a tree
For days!' bubbled Hobden: 'when in the name
Of God and King will we put an end to this?'
     But then the cooper came
With more: 'We just got this: Three hundred horse
Surprised in a forest glade. Apparently

Some thousand sovereign taken. No
Deaths.' 'A th– a th– a th–' the men
Contributed: 'T-t-t-taken where?'
     'No one knows. But a green
Leaf was found nearby the place.' 'There,
I warned you,' hissed the fletcher, 'I did so!'

They stood in growing silence, growing what
Silence grows. 'What will the man do next?'
'Who knows, he has shown himself entirely without
     Scruple: he clearly attacks
Even the worthiest, noblest men and will flout
Every Law of the land. Manifestly not

An Englishman.' They muttered and dispersed
Towards their tensing women. The sun came out.
Way up in Nottinghamshire the sun went in
     And a staggered, spreading shout
Rose from the tiniest homes, where every bin
Yielded an amber sovereign, and the worst

Befalling on that day was a light shower.
The worst that week a couple of colds. The kids
Compared dates on their coins and showed the women.
     The elders looked to the clouds
Every day, but the dimmest blinked at the bowmen
They were sure they saw in the tops of the trees. An hour

Later Hobden and several hundred men
Found what they were looking for: a wood.
They neighed and dismounted, flattened a useless chart
     They thought they understood,
And rubbed their hands and made an early start,
Watching the ground, heading towards the glen.

In Herrick Shape for Her

Between the ranges of their sleeps
   They churn arriving light,
   The Burnt-out, the Despite,
The muffled in their homes and heaps,
   A woman on her own:
The swarf of spinning markets, who,
   Worn, dreading, blown,
   Do all they have to do.

London's now where what is cold
   Is terminal. And what
   Does not succeed does not
Survive. Alleys are clogged, filled,
   The circulating breath
Reproaches who exhaled it, pain
   Cavils at the teeth,
   Jerks the blinking brain

To unrecorded ticks of keen
   And obvious desire.
   The lady was a liar
Who blared from the unblurring screen
   Home truths of the Great British;
A truth is that what's muttered by
   The woman by the rubbish
   Is not 'I yearn to die.'

Meantime the capable delight
   In edibles elsewhere;
   The million-copied hair
Crowns the coy and poising sight
   Of Beauty for the week.
But that was it, the measured-out
   Proportion of this work
   It merits. That was it.

More than it. So poll me: who
    Will gauge the gap between
    The drool of the obscene
Gogettable, the selling show
    That celebrates in space –
And the discarded kind who, miles
    Out of the dog race,
    Litter these flogged isles

And live? Show me another many,
    Many sure of less,
    Of losses, otherness,
And of the Grand Perhaps. Money
    Zips his bag at this,
Crosses the human out and flies
    To where more Money is.
    No loss that: nothing dies

In us at that. For in her time
    And more than abstract noun,
    Love works, and with a frown
Of homing thought remembers I'm
    Waiting, so she writes
The name of nothing but this place,
    Travels a while and sits.
    I hold the hands she has.

We hold that only certainty
    While certain it is none,
    And, as we hold, what's done
Is done for only money. We
    Divined from where we held:
We saw the slurping addict led
    Down to the red hold,
    Treated, dealt and fed,

Drained of all contrariwise,
    Impoverished, unseen,
    Met squinting at a screen,
With silver oblongs for the eyes
    So terribly impressed.
We turn from what was lost to what
    Is left: at the cool least
    These sheets, us in your flat,

Home from the sound. Dear, reread
  The yellowest of books.
  The night is black and looks
Like nothing. We are what we need:
  Ahead leans our Enough,
Its novelties of whim and care,
  While our inwit – that Love
  Might, fountaining from here,

Wash far towards the negligible,
  Trickle up to those
  Who hug their only clothes,
Whose breath is now so tangible
  It rots them – rests its head
On London's cold and toppling height
  And clears, in every bed,
  Its throat for the whole fight.

Perigueux

With give or take a hundred years to build the high wall
To save beloveds from the Goths, the Vandals, them all,
 Who do come, they tear apart
 Their one cathedral.

They pull the wings of theatres off, the sides of their homes;
Monuments they ruin, towers and spires, green domes,
 Are picked to bits to build the wall
 To stop what comes.

But it's yawn-work, a century passed manly in the sun,
With long leisure, quarrels, doubts, little getting done
 For months, as rocks are rolled and piled
 And the Isle flows on.

You still see what a feeble piecemeal mess of it they made,
The Men of Perigueux, as if not all that afraid:
 You see old stones from older things
 Jumbled in shade

Now, now, in '91, and 19', not 9':
The Ostrogoths, the Vikings, English, everybody's line
 Overran this place and tore
 Everything down.

Still, someone picks his tools up, gets on with the slow task.
Carries rocks an afternoon, helps out after dusk.
 Puts an hour or two in, knows
 What's at risk,

Even though he and his children, their children, theirs,
Won't be around to man the walls or barricade the stairs
 When strain or terror take this city
 Unawares.

Seventh Day

My tiredness was mine, my fault, my harm.
Saturday day-and-night was wild and skinned me.
I woke to the worst, laughing, stung,
I mean I was raw, light red, and out and facing
        another Sunday.

All the clear good deeds of drinks: water,
seltzer, milk, orange, lime, a single
apologetic beer by my avid lunch
and dark enjoying company of challenge,
        flirt, mingle –

were not enough when aloneness, lethal
and newer than love stood up and took me away.
Sat me in places bubbled with light, fear,
and huge quiet. A human, topped by thick hair,
        stuck with me.

Tried to remember and read, but the *vertigo*!
Hoped to mention and phone, but 'a hundred years'!
Glimpsed programmes, parents, my done Saturday
moaning still: 'It rolls, it rocks!' the Sunday:
        'It disappears.'

So dark appeared, September's, sudden, damp.
Not for very much longer the vivid excessive
awareness – had hoped to jog or phone but no.
Only the getting through and rid of the dead slow
        suffered, passive

seventh day of the last, I mean latest, seven.
Lacking a skin, as I always put it to someone.
If she says one vowel it's the onset of all
care, all cure. More than that syllable
        wrecks, and a hard one

saps and threatens the tree I am, the I am.
Weaker than any citizen, more vital,
only vital, in fact, and breathing to bed
I lie without rest, warm and think the unsaid
        and age my little

age, awake. Well I had to sit up as a ghost
and gather a curtain and sash up the window – there
the safe and orange satellite town, my world
shut and remotely loving, its subject singled,
      framed, bare,

receding, reaching to water,
sighing out to a drawer where the single pill
slips and ensures the end of endured sabbath,
freezes the light, stops its everything
      but the moon on the sill.

Nativity

Town of a hundred thousand hands
Locks in for snow. The sky goes somehow
Orange and green, orange *and* green
    As the animals go where animals go:
    Away, behind, due south, below.

Flaring in freshening welcome dusk
Like matches struck the Nativities glow,
Curl in the sight of arriving boy,
    Chorusing parent, mouthing girl,
    Stressed and entire the infant world.

The mirrors are framed with the lights they mirror:
They people and double the rooms with infinite
Manifestations of a bright none other.
    'For one to appear!' cries someone there,
    So close to expecting it, eyes to the air.

Moments when what no longer matters
Is actually Time and incredibly Money
Visit on towns of ten to ten million,
    Swoop like a targeting bird from an eyrie,
    As furiously quickly, as over, as scary.

Who saw it all stamp. Over the writer
Hovers that quiet that started as answer,
Aged to a question, ended as quiet
    But sensed, as the animal everywhere sense
    Sudden, distinct, involving events.

Apocrypha

The nets were full without the saints
who slithered out between the chance
gospels. One beyond that book
rose up beside the real brook
so full of fish a man could poise
and balance. Small as hearts of boys
at birth, he grew, believed each shrub
a wood and soon each wood a shrub.

When only young he dwarfed our dead
volcano, and he left for good,
to wander, reason, reckon, work:
that he'd be lucky, that he'd be back
we never felt, and we were right.
From time to time, some milky night
we think, colossally above,
one hug is answered with enough,

but oftener, when days are long,
the horseman right, the village wrong,
the market rigged, the warrant signed,
this is the saint we bring to mind,
or try, as if we thought a saint
would pace the world, true, silent,
seeing nothing. Or nothing we
ourselves for Christ's sake couldn't see.

The World Unity Organisation Workers

Flags as white as if they never meant
remotely to be victors, white armbands
as if to note they really carry feathers
and wish the world to know it, the World
Unity Organisation Workers kneel
    and do their business, while

Our Lads slap and sweat, are lit with pride
in utterances of utmost energy
beamed home to the ready for the parade.
I do not think we need to be, and are not,
informed the sky is poisonous to all
    intents and purposes

forever, nor that the generation melted
may have been timid, reading types, or boastful
centre-forwards, sons, drummers, drunks.
It seems we owe the flames the only thanks
flaring forth, and meanwhile the World
    Unity Organisation

Workers squat and bandage, knot, explain,
or build, out of shot. A household name
may walk with the perspiring Press on a tour
of lads who didn't melt, with their thumbs up,
written to by a whole sex of a homeland,
    may perch in a tank's top,

swivel around for the rapt electorates
and climb; but apart, the World Unity
Organisation Workers work on what-
ever it is they do who are on no side,
were of no help at all, yet expect to reap
    the harvests we reap.

And Leaves Astonishing

For now, among the falling of the ochres,
Reds and yellows, in which haze the many
    Casualties of what on earth
Went on here this month, re-fuse, this joker's
Pockets open out and he digs for money.

His the face suggested to, spat on,
In which the door and final door were shut,
    The mother of which saw and lost
At stations, and the quizzes of the Western
Shows made to a shape you don't forget:

Human of the Revolution, soul
We would wouldn't we be if our dreams
    Loomed amateur cine of tanks
Slowing round our corner and the whole
Hope thing holed and fumbling in own homes –

For now he buys and smokes and his rivered mug
Grins above the inhalation. It all
    Rustles by beyond him now,
The elbowing to run the show, the lag
Of bloody onus, economic stall,

The eloquence and begging in the States
And books of what it was, means, portends.
    Photographed and asked, he moves
His hand to – what, to offer cigarettes
Nobody takes. He takes and lights one, stands

And leaves, astonishing the siding rich
With just being. The love sticks on the tongue.
    He goes his way, who went his way,
Where talk is meant and lit, at the throat's hutch,
On streets of blood, in cafés of the lung.

Didymus the Seated

Without a shadow of doubt,
Debate on Whether or Not has ad infinitum
Filled to the roof an auditorium: risen
Velveted podia, strung an array of mikes
As if for a leisurely doo-wop over the footlights
      Of a hired Victorian stage;

But in this blurting age,
More to the taste of the open holes of the horde
Is a boom, a spot, a cue, a one word roared,
Repeated, roared, chanted, sung to a drum
Or klaxoned over a sloping sea of foam
      Until it's all there is.

From time to time to this
Comes one who outwrinkles most by his or her
Inclination to frown or to crinkle, or
Otherwise to do what is other than gaze with love,
Cry real tears, want what you have to have,
      Or join in the deafening noise

To make the obedient choice.
He or she or once in a blue moon them
Can share in the field of silence after the storm,
Keeping their thinking hushed in the crypt of selves
While the world's liars accomplish nothing by halves,
      Or they can be the one

Insufferable citizen
Who multiplies life anew by the any question
That turns the globe of the screamingly loving a system
Back to a stage and a measly being whose job
Is trying to be very big and have a club.
      Remember, St Thomas,

The Disciple Didymus,
Was alone not in his being the only one
To disbelieve without proof (the other ten
Had seen: they had no choice but to believe):
But left in the cave he furrowed his brow with love
     And wondered with reason.

In this mendacious season,
Find the compelled attentive child who is staring
Not at the idol but at the standing cheering.
Do not disturb or remove him from his chair.
Tiptoe in jeans up the aisle and say in his ear:
     There is a saint for doubt.

Springs of Simon Peter

In a town in which to have tried three times
he rose and he spent such afternoons
    between his friends,
    at Jim's and Tom's
and out, having so chuckled of each
to the other he'd never be out of touch.

Days were for blame and invite; nights
were many though he could have had more, he reckoned,
    and every second
    was up in lights
but he tottered home and peered at his board
for messages, and the word was LORD.

And then it was blank and always so,
a tabula rasa coloured lavender
    only. The calender
    had less to show
as he riffled it forwards. Here came Jim
but he'd gone by then, when here came Tom.

The next fresh four a.m. he was treading
deazil around the Lake and the thought
    in his head was what
    he was clearly reading
on stones, dates and pages, an ache
to hear, register, shiver, and speak

to stranger and stranger, mentioned, shunned,
a punchline: he would wait in the dust
    all night for the first
    and freezing sound
of the barracking cock, and a surge of sudden
what? then home to his hissing garden

and huge, turning keys. In a town
in which to have tried three times he would lie
    as the very day
    would break, with his fawn
long arms hiding the falls of his face
from his own words spreading through the whole of space.

Thief on the Cross

How are you doing on yours, my pal
in crime? Are you off where the hurt has hurt so far
    it's what life is, and before
was all the goners like us will ever cop
    of paradiso? Well?

Or are you flapping away in the three
agonies, my apprentice? Is that what
    fixes your look on the flat
world we were caught and tried in, makes you turn
    lollingly from me?

Why ever it is − is it your lips?
dry as the lot will be by the squawking dawn,
    dusty as all by noon? −
you've barely cracked a word in our lingo since
    that tin-tiled cyclops

pegged us to our final form,
condemned by imperial thieves to peg as thieves,
    unmissed. Those wailing wives
are crawling back to the feet of our mate in front:
    that triples the hurt for him

in any case. I'm glad we two
purloined a moment's peace from the long pain
    it turned into. Not again −
you're going to ask him again, aren't you? Aren't you
    satisfied? I tell you,

feckless snivelling rascal whelp:
we're only smack bang where our blessed old dears
    predicted, all those years
gone: but this one isn't one of us lot.
    He's innocent; he can't help.

Tale of the Crimson Team

I

For they were the leading team, and they met at about
Ten this morning, and filed up into their coach.
They were known for their crimson colour, the dog on the shirt
Rampant, as they say, or 'rampant', as they said.
They had a song, and by the time
The Manager, scarved, was standing up by the Driver
And trying to wave the noise down they were singing it,
Though by the time they finished the whole
Party was out in the countryside, and the singing was
Settling back to yawns and a little silence.
Some were just about sleeping, and even the five
At the very back were smoking or looking out,
I-spying cars with crimson stars in the quarterlights,
Shocking a passenger with who they were
And how relaxed they seemed! whose favourite colour
Was known to every boy and was always crimson.
The passenger would never forget those seconds.
For the Crimson Team were the best on all of the islands,
And on their way to a distant town to prove it,
As they had proved it time and time again,
To all proud cities and the upstart towns, in
Sweat and sun, in filths and rain, at night,
In other hemispheres and another decade.
And this game? Workaday, to be honest, a chore!
Well almost, just a matter of getting there
And doing the business, as they put it. The players
Had plans for the evening, back in their own places,
Each the bull of a clubnight's foaming love,
Far from rivals and the inept defeated.
Today's opponents would play in an ivy green.
Something to do with the history of their hole,
That colour. Not exactly the Rampant Crimson,
Was it. They hadn't a snowball in hell, that shower,
Known for their sallow faces and dissent.
And they played at a rotting ground in industrial wind.
 – Made the Crimson wonder why they bothered,
The Ivy Greens, when they could spend the same time

Say, fishing, out of harm's way, like good boys,
Instead of stumbling again round their own ground.
They were almost as bad as the Blue lot, that
Arrogant and hustling mob of ex-
Bootroom boys they'd humbled last week,
Or the local Pinks, exponents of the kick,
Whom they'd dutifully upended on the last
Day of the last season. Not to mention that
Brown-and-Yellow hooped and cheating gang:
Unprofessionals. The Crimson sang
The songs of the dim shame of all opponents.
They were in fine voice in the sun: it was elevenish.
The Number 1, the old hand, was back on form
With anecdotes of the knackered old heroes
They'd all grown up on. The Numbers 11 and 12
Started the usual jokes to the usual groans.
The fields went by at their pace and the hurtling road
Flew on at its faster pace. The Number 5
Looked to the faraway villages and hoped
What he always hoped, checking his bag again.
A fixed opinion struck the Number 10,
(He'd kept his aisle-seat, among so many men),
While the Number 4 suggested the game they never
Tired of playing but couldn't get it going this time:
They all seemed almost in awe
Of the brightness that flooded the coach, cresting them all
With daylight, lightening them, as if the aspect
Of their excellence was making itself visible,
Appearing as a – blond light, an admission that
None would ever better them, none *could* ever.
The Number 7, the youngster, tipped for a place
In a team to play the Rest of the World this summer,
Woke from a dream of that and broke the silence
With the question 'What's with the silence?'
And if you call this an answer the Number 3
Turned from the window and said 'This ain't the way.'
The motorway did seem empty, for a motorway:
No bridges, pylons, now no markings either.
The Manager confided to the Driver
He didn't recognise the country. The Driver
Turned to the Manager, smiled and confided
He didn't recognise the country either.

II

Come up on this cloud, friend – you know who you are
And this isn't forever, make yourself comfy there –
Peer down at the moving veins of the land.
You haven't the vertigo I have. I have to
Rope myself to this solider nimbus here;
But look at the traffic inching along where it is.
Does it all have someone to hate or beat or both?
You imagine so. I imagine so too.
Something to always know, always do.
The islands are lacerated with that today, that
Feeling, as if the great heat hatched it alive,
Sniffling along from its home to its enemy's.
The roads are blinding, the bare-headed sweat in the lay-by,
Directing to destinations each will duly
Scorn and spare no effort to overrun.
Loyalty will be bloody; menace fun.
Chants will be crude and easy to memorise,
There will be no arbiter, quarter or compromise,
And the victory will be bugled home as a merited
Fair ransacking – any shock, impossible loss
A falsehood or concealed. There will be no gain
That's not for good. Down the unwinding lane
Crawls that lonely coach which is following
Only it. Where is it going? Not home:
Somebody else's home to dishearten it,
Sadden its working self with a loaded luck
And leave it. It streams its colour behind it, its hour
Is only that, its colour its colour for what.
They're only games, and this is only that.
But as such, watch it with me, focus upon
The coach of the unison of hoping males,
Losing itself in this place where nothing's to play,
Where it isn't necessarily day or night-time,
Where no one will shout at odds or accuse or cheat them,
There is no plan to embarrass, blame or defeat them,
And nothing they risk will blunder into its obverse.
                                                    No,

The bright unoffended fields will be waiting, swaying,
Shushed, for the coach to come to its standstill by them;
For the Driver to shrug at the Manager, as if the
Silence of his own men was what had stopped them,

For player to glance at player and give away nothing
One could infer as fear but to turn away
Chewing, to confirm that as far as the eye could blink
Or believe were somebody's fields and the motorway
Had come to nothing there. Whose fields they were
Was nowhere to be seen.
                                    The fields were wheatfields.
And those, further and redder with, no, poppies?
Hardly, not now. While yes, a gust of life, a
Blurring aeroplane wake, long underlining
Its white forgetting that it was ever noise.

The coach door opens and glints as they file out.
Against the numb horizon they make these plans:
Food, a party to quest for and question the first
Local they find. Number 1 to get to a phone.
If he must he will talk to men of the distant town
They came to outflank and fool. He will first say 'wait'.
He will choose his words. He will finally say 'help'.
He will gaze at the coach and its disappointed cargo.

They will don their crimson strip with the printed dogs
To show solidarity. Some will strike up the song.
The Numbers 11 and 12 will come into their own
At last as jokers, putting the Manager's scarf on
To cheers and shouts for a change. The young Number 7s
Dream will be longer and slower towards its end.
A different view will occur to the Number 10.
The Number 5 will be long-gone by then.
The Manager and the Driver will learn each other's
Histories, and from them, and those at the back
Will share what's left of the Marlboros.
                                    The wind
Will bustle its great way across the fields,
Green, yellowish, reddish fields and flutter
The hair on the forehead of every player, that wind,
And whisk the clouds in front of the setting sun,
And peel the clouds away from the rising sun
Until they are found, if they're ever found, a team
Who knew the tricks, who played in beautiful
Crissing patterns they worked on on floodlit nights
In sevens, lightning threes and incredible twos,
And never believed they would lose, and, at the last,
Believed they would never lose.

Historian

Only for some other can you stand
   on a horizon. Never for your own
look. There is a fresh rain on the hinterland.

You, Historian, read and breathe alone
   on this green lane. You came with no belief,
only delight, hazel eyes, and a patient brain.

Here where a border hung, in the other life,
   the trees go by, the animals discuss
at fair length, even the space declares its love

for who will not destroy it, and the moss
   flows across the stone and the air drips.
Monuments alone record the monumental loss.

The question on your lips
   is quietened by how, in increasing light,
something in the wind begins and lightly steps

into your very sight,
   and a foreign dance begins to which you are wholly
welcome in the dew, you, who stand with only delight,

hazel eyes and a patient brain and truly
   undecided look. Historian,
you have arrived beside what is a nursery,

and like a nursery where who would govern
   is stuck for good elsewhere, huge in a bottle,
you have arrived in your own son's idea of heaven,

and mine when you were little.
   Now mummers spiral from unbroken land;
the memory of a wire, endless indistinct gun-metal,

dissolves into a movement of one hand
   into a second hand, a ring is forming,
connecting only everything, the mountain, the old sand

it ended, and whoever else is coming
    joins on, surprised, for no good reason
other than the sun. But again, in the blue evening,

    a righteous head will take up the horizon
        with wire for hair, and glare a terrible fill
until what is not what he is is frozen.

    The tired historian sinks to the dead hill.
        The air stops like music.
The last wildly spinning pine gulps, and is still.

Deep Song of Us

The slowness of this thought: the rocky street.
The white and slowness of these fingers: meat
    Afloat. The utterable word
    Gulped, the plausible self
Clammed, in hiding. Booms of a heart unheard
    Impel this head, this whole head,
        Towards a gulf.

High over, far below, the being beats
Onward, habited, drummed, and light repeats
    It isn't its opposite.
    The seconds reel along
On six enclosing films, and the next minute
    Forms into a room, this room,
        For this song.

We are the underwater here, the cold
Progressors from elsewhere, from gaps in an old
    Silence to new gaps
    In a fresh silence: still,
We eat, will not unsip the monster sips
    Of the wide blue, the narrow blue,
        Unbreathing chill.

Look how the brown bewitcher looms into view,
Startled but only startled by how you
    Stared at her. The drapes
    Settle across that sight.
Along the world's great side three fluttering shapes
    Could be tracking us. Could be luring us.
        Could bite.

We are the underwater. Do you blame us?
Do you know us? Do you really. Name us.
    Tell us by our twin
    Terrors: one, these yellow
Gleaming aliens hauling our kind in,
    The spit of us, the salt of us,
        Our fellow;

Then, rainbow-rimmed, the lidding placid sky,
Unswallowable except to surface and die
         On heaven sauced with thick
         Floats. We agree hell
The better deal, and lump together, sick.
         I reckon this. You reckon this.
                  It's just as well,

For the front line is a horror. Now all lines
Are horrors: a child dapples, flashes, shines –
         We say Get down. Dive.
         Plunge and forget, yawn
That jaw then sip in shadow, still alive,
         Sunlight-proof. Midnight-proof.
                  Immune to dawn.

We hit the bottom, watch our gravely ill
Lug themselves towards us, and we know we'll
         Kick to the green middle,
         Hang out there for a spell,
An inturned, peering, recognising huddle:
         You three and me. You six and me.
                  What do we tell –

Catch my eyes I tell an embedded tale
Of one and another one, female and male
         Slipped together: Ring-
         And-Finger. This goes down
In silence by our firesides but we sing
         A song then. The song then.
                  Around our town.

We sing where the whole schools of the sky-eyed green
Chew, reminded. We sing by the machine
         That somersaulted slowly,
         Falling through everything,
Chains elbowing down and past our holy
         Quiet, landing in quiet,
                  Balancing,

And finally caving over into the sand.
We sing by what was a ship, and what a hand.
    We sing where light and smell
    Mean danger and the other,
And call our hell a heaven for a hell.
    We repeat bits. We repeat bits
        To one another.

I save my best bass for the brown bewitcher
When she comes, but when she does I'll watch her
    In deep, wide hunger
    And lose my place, I know.
And not a few will hear my Ring-and-Finger
    And doubt it, doubt I believe it.
        I do, though.

Inaudible, we sing. Misunderstood
We do the seven actions. If you only could
    See us you would know.
    Over the oil in the sky,
Where both our diehards and our light dead go,
    Where you paint us, where you want us,
        Where you don't die,

Where you walk on, your each mutter a scream
To our ears, your scream a wordless scream,
    Our colours yours, though yours
    We blend to the one lime,
Your toxin steeping down into our pores
    Forever, to ring forever,
        Ingested time:

You would know that – Hunt us, clouds will clear.
Catch us, one held dear will hold you dear.
    Roast us, we will trust.
    Waste us in the heaven
You hope is hell, and we shall be at rest:
    Do what you do. Whatever you do,
        You stay forgiven.

Short Lyrics

1. *Rumplestiltskin*

'Your name is Rumplestiltskin!' cried
The Queen. 'It's not,' he lied. 'I lied
The time you heard me say it was.'
'I never heard you. It's a guess,'

She lied. He lied: 'My name is Zed.'
She told the truth: 'You're turning red,
Zed.' He said: 'That's not my name!'
'You're turning red though, all the same.'

'Liar!' he cried: 'I'm turning blue.'
And this was absolutely true.
And then he tore himself in two,
As liars tend to have to do.

2. *Song to the Skinhead*

'Ginger, you are going to die.'
I am, but was that what you meant
that summer night you cycled by
while I was on my steady way
home and watched you pedal away
    not watching where I went?

I haven't yet. What did you mean?
You haven't either. Yes, I'd know
– I'd even care – but I haven't seen
your mugshot on a local page
with how or when you went, your age,
    or where the wreaths should go.

We're older now. You haven't said
a word since 'You are going to die'
(to me, I mean) and well, we've led
extremely different kinds of lives
since. I haven't carried knives.
    You probably don't sigh.

But well, I will say this. There are some
moments from the time they are
until the time we're not, that come
and never weaken, never fade,
and you created one that stayed
    and will, like any star:

'Ginger, you are going to die,'
you said, and biked into the blue.
For that, and that I haven't, I –
thankyou. When I need to know
that any can be loved, I do
    tend to begin with you.

3. *Audition Piece*

It isn't in your blood. What do you know.
You never acted in your life. You say.
Your mates are good, they're funny, they'll have a go.
You'll come and see it, though. You go away.

A day passes, a night and it's Wednesday.
All but you enquire and all but you
Pout to be told as little as yesterday,
And you I see little of, though in the queue

For lunch you look away. You tend to.
I noticed when you read for me, your eyes
Were either on the page or on the blue
Inside of your folder. Should they rise

I'll look away myself. Now I hear cries.
I pinned my choices on the wall. 'At last!'
Has given way to mutters of surprise,
But tough. You were perfect. You are cast.

4. *The Perfect Match*

There is nothing like the five minutes to go:
Your lads one up, your lads one down, or the whole
    Thing even. How you actually feel,
        What you truly know,
Is that your lads are going to do it. So,

However many times in the past the fact
Is that they didn't, however you screamed and strained,
    Pummelled the floor, looked up and groaned
        As the Seiko ticked
On, when the ultimate ball is nodded or kicked

The man in the air is you. Your beautiful wife
May curl in the corner yawningly calm and true,
    But something's going on with you
        That lasts male life.
Love's one thing, but this is the Big Chief.

5. *And the Next*

I had a conversation
With the next generation,
And they said 'Quit smoking'
And they weren't joking.

6. *What she will include*

What she will include
in all her letters from the south
will come as no surprise,
but be attractive to such eyes
as rested on her mouth
   in the cold mood.

Within the interim,
that tucked silence plus the red
small ball of hardened thought:
why the dismissal, that retort,
why any curt thing said
   to her by him?

Only the hope that merely
to split and clear and allow to grow
in one eventual room,
ramifying and bound to bloom,
the strain this rich and slow,
    daily, yearly.

7. *The Great*

Climb in in the cold.
It's the best way to bed.
The younger ones are old,
The old ones dead,

The even older stand
And sit when you sit.
They wish to warm your cold hand
But are burned by it.

8. *Read over long time*

If we did not merit
Our months together,
We deserved neither
The absence after,
The having to bear it
But that's what we have:
The doubting letter
And the doubted love.

Or what we had then.
Everyone other
Than you and this lover
Has passed, not seen,
The whiteness between
One line and another.
For the absence has been,
Is over, as never.

But follow no further.
The whiteness is growing
A god, unwriting
And poised wherever
The colours wither.
The trick is doing,
While the light is going,
Its awful favour.

Foreseeable horror
Climbs in the weather.
That it can do.
I will love you
In many and few
Words, as this blue
Will reach out blacker,
Be done forever.

Reappear, smoother
Than paper, than other.
Young alongside,
From the date to the bride
Remain, though neither
The ear and this heard
Nor eye and this word
Last out together.

9. *The Captain of the Past*

He was the Captain of the Past
Who sailed in the locked Ship
That haunted its high Self
With him across the Hours
Who rode across the Waves
That broke on where she now
Shells and cooks alone.

For Crew he had the Cabin
And Sameness of the Books
That Helm and his scroll-coloured
Skin and the old Cap
That tilted from the tall Head
Which lowered to its Sleep
Upon the accurate Map.

And the Sea-Miles pour past
And Knots plunge and swell
In nightly violet Distances
Looking like those Hoseheads
Whom no one will believe
Who steps towards the Captain
In other Time than Past.

He woke and he was working
The decks of the locked Ship
That leaned into the Westerly
Or he believed it leaned
Who rolled a beloved Map
And was the undisputed Captain
Of the towering Ship.

10. *Venus lights the mauve Horizon*

Yet shipping rain the trough
Encumbering England starts
To wheel and spirals off

So stars are out these nights
High over where I live.
It must be Venus lights

The mauve horizon. I've
Fallen for that trick
That isn't one. I love

One. I bear my luck
And have it. In the east
Is held the honouring cloak

For these shoulders, vast
And patient as it settles
About them in the west.

11. *Believe that this*

Believe that this
believed it twice,
doubted it twice
and still believes

either and both
unmarrying truths,
mirroring yesses
in halls of guesses

and you will know,
dear, when you are
and kiss, how this
and all we bless

was done, is done,
will be, had been,
whether intended,
needed or fallen

to vein or ion,
by power or person
for love or lesson
of hell or heaven.

12. *Poem in blank rhyme*

This isn't very difficult to do.
The sky's pink, the morning pretty new.

Last night I met a mate from the old crew.
We walked too far too late and turned a U

Out of the woods as it got dark. He knew
I'd spend the evening talking about you

But didn't mind and, when we had to queue,
He made the time fly quickly with his two

Dozen unfunny jokes, plus a big clue
About his own big heart. Well the sky's blue

Now over there, I'm standing in the dew,
Remembering and hoping. But it's true:

Days are very many. Days are few.
I want to be with someone and you're who.

Look a Rainbow

That scholar saw himself
as any of many classical figures: in some
difficulty, derided upon a plain,
or dodging the giant swoop of the foreshadowed
loathing bird, or turning uphill again,
or swivelling in lace too lovely to be trusted,
or being among the men
picked or being the loser plumping for gold;

there was not a mythical bod, whether young or old,
marvelling or smug,
chameleon or merman he couldn't see
himself as in a way, and said so. I,
charioted through this town by friends,
loves and relatives on the other hand,
saw him rarely, saw him precisely when
with no thing left to be learned and I mean no thing,

he looked through the one pane at the passing city
and looked, for all the world, like a man beginning
on knowledge, any knowledge, new, alone
with his had food and dead slow-winking moon
first hinting to him, equably dim plainsman,
at a god who wasn't God and might be no one.
No one
looked hollower than the thinker then, who would rise

into a world he could treat as types of Oxford:
Creation from Christ Church to Blackbird Leys
of the unnoticed streets; Cowley
the hammering that has to happen; Binsey
the little heaven. He would note and rise
into the rustling spectrum his own god
or innocent as one, as culpable,
as impossible or as cloaked a likelihood,

and set his mind to rights by how
it looked. It looked, now, like an age of flux,
now like a borne-out prophecy of his,
now like a day for red wine, frank sex,
now like his podium, now like his tiger pit.
But he – it has to be said, and I'm saying it –
for all this fixity, which I as an angel
deem hilarious and, as a man, amusing,

was not, at any rate,
literally lethal. For that, get a load of this:
a true believer photographed in a tank;
a diehard with an okaying imp on his shoulder;
a demagogue home and scorned in bed, with a brother
jealous of pity and rising to judge the pleading;
a rags to riches to righteous man
setting down his four – three – two-point Plan;

an industrialist hedging in his turret;
three in a line assuring you and twitching
as they call news lies and they blame numbers;
a self-made man who states in a perfect world
the dead could have come this far;
a promiser of zero; a created
Lord with a herding instinct; safe Christians
calling for hanging humans as those humans

dial back today, and a man-of-the-people
not technically lying to you. They –
and let me get this right – believed that they
did not, would not, could not, do wrong, and they
marched on the land like that,
sons of the number one,
spawn of a single possible colour,
animated alone by coinage, as

opposed to the numbers two to over four billion,
colours darker and paler than theirs to the ends
of the rainbow, as opposed
to any sounds but those of a piling profit,
and any visions but rolls
of instructing paper and mounds of the runniest gold.
If the above most knowledgeable man in the wide world
could look as wholly void when fondly imagining,

imagine how these looked, who could see but one
view, hear but one truth, and smell
nigh on everything alien – it's a way
to look at it, and I, who can count beyond
two, and have found new ways to impress the beloved
since and know a rainbow when I see
a fucking rainbow, and hear what floats by me,
am seeing it that way now, though I do not need

to be infinite with pity, or sitting
with my whitesox feet dangling out over the side
of this constantly-changing-colour aurora
to see it that way – albeit that's what I'm up to
as we speak: I could drop towards the quietest
nook of the Bod and tell my creation 'Listen:
this is the winged "Or" ', or I could glide by
the strongest leader's weightless spiralling head

and whisper 'Or' some several years before
our nation or historian or assassin
takes it up. (As far as the word "or" goes,
the brass might thank me when the desperate finger
poises to dial the O that clicks and causes
a civil war or too-close-to-call election.) I
would give new life to the mocked compound "yesman",
that it might instead denote

those who far from oiling a furious engine
designed to allow the one thing and not the next thing,
are children, women and men (we say 'yesperson')
who when, in the bulletin glare, or going to the wall,
or at the martyred murderer's grave,
or hearing the chant for nightmare to befall
who isn't chanting, or sniffing the burning alive
what only grows, only grows, would

let, into their rainbow-including eyes,
the other lights and it's this
that slows and qualifies their steady breaths
and long thought-out replies. Their lives
would spell yes, y-e-s, their deaths
would be unembittered fadings, and their acts
waltz puzzlingly beyond the flagged checkpoints
of mired, miserable sticklers;

they would be among the best pals of the man
at the beginning (now he walks on St Aldates)
whether he wanted or no, and he doesn't know
that, does he? but equally
they would be among the best pals of his equal
who gapes in an appalling Crimean
orphanage, or drools on Eritrea,
and of course, of course,

they would hope to be invited when the two
meet, and the less likely that they will,
the more they do. Ah well,
I see the scholar pass away down Pembroke Street,
knowing everything he knows. But I
could reach The Perch by noon, or The Trout by two,
where the peacocks are, or get right out to the country,
make a day of it, if I really do fly.